# Seventies Child And Other Fashion Trends

Brendan Hawthorne

**SEVENTIES CHILD AND OTHER FASHION TRENDS**



First Printing: 2021

ISBN: 978-1-7399337-1-5 (DREAM WELL WRITING LTD)

DREAM WELL WRITING LTD
STAFFORDSHIRE
UNITED KINGDOM

www.dreamwellwriting.simplesite.com

DREAM WELL

A Dyslexia Friendly Publication

# *Seventies Child and Other Fashion Trends*

# DEDICATION

This book is dedicated to: Lynn, my wife - critic, proofreader and putter upper of artistic challenges!

To my mom for being a voice of reason.

To Kerry, my partner in music, for being a true friend and to Ferdinand the Cat for lending a paw, sharing his view on life and his cat Zen approach to dealing with the 21$^{st}$ century.

To all of those people who have been there for me over the years and to those I am yet to meet on this poetic odyssey, this is for you! x

# CONTENTS

These are poems that may help save your life!

Turn to them when feeling lost and misunderstood.

Turn to them when the whole world has gone mad.

Turn to them when you don`t know how to articulate what`s in your soul.

Turn to them if wondering whether anyone else has ever passed this way because they have and lived to tell the tale.

Turn to these poems because they may just save your life.

They saved mine.

Ian Henery

## Writing in the Sky

### (A dream of my childhood, for Oliver Postgate)

He saw the small things
scurrying around in other dimensions
Parallel marvels with a story to tell
So he gave them a stage
a medium
a form
that kept me warm
under the sleepy blankets of my childhood
that flickered with coal fire shadows
and black and white transmissions
I invested my youth
in the Dragons' Friendly Society
before journeying out through space
to small planets
inhabited by hand-knitted aliens
who whooped and simply cared for each other
I crashed through the waves on longship sagas
imbibed moral strength and goodness
and then ran and ran through Pogles' Wood
with Pippin and Tog
where we drank tea with plants
under skies filled with
dandelion heads and umbrellas

And now as my belly sags
like an old cloth cat
I miss the man I never knew
The one who made
my early years magic
by keeping me on the rails
with well-oiled tank engines
and small films
And now in my old age
I'm left understanding
the bravery of an artistic
Red Cross man
who walked out
into the horrors of battle
and brought back peace
security
and a sense of belonging
to pass from generation
to generation
And now he has left us
left us with a legacy of brilliance
that was born in a shed
somewhere between
Hendon and Broadstairs
Sleep my old friend
while I weep for your loss

The loss of a man I never knew
who made my childhood complete
with paper
wool and string
and the shelter of an outstretched
metallic wing

# NOTE FROM THE EDITOR

It has been an absolute pleasure to work with Brendan on the editing and publication of his most recent poetry collection. Many of the pieces have made me smile, in recognition, from hearing them at Brendan's spoken word performances. It is a privilege to be able to take the time to read and analyse the text and to get to know the various stories and inspirations behind the poetry in this collection.

Brendan has kept me on my toes in his use of Black Country lexis and I have found it interesting to learn more about these, and to see the way Brendan's writing style evolves from earlier pieces selected for the first sections of this book – some of which were first written around twenty years ago – through to his most recent work in Part Five.

I absolutely love Brendan's most recently written pieces, such as Glass Swans, which presents such beautiful imagery in amongst the everyday, and I have thoroughly enjoyed journeying back to the 1970s in poems such as High Rise Living (Going Up) to see the frustrations and tribulations of life from the perspective of a *Seventies Child*...

Mel Wardle Woodend

Staffordshire Poet Laureate 2019 – 2022 and
Director of Dream Well Writing Ltd

# ACKNOWLEDGEMENTS

I wish to thank all of the friends, audiences and organisations that have supported me over the years.

I would like to thank Bluechrome for seeking me out in the first place and publishing my first book back in 2004.

Massive thanks to Geoff Stevens and Dave Reeves for sharing their writing experiences with me over the years and for helping shape a novice writer into what he is today!

# INTRODUCTION

This volume of poems spans twenty years of writing and as I am now in the year of my sixtieth birthday I thought it was about time for a 'Best of' and 'This is me now' compilation.

Many of my early collections are hard to find and out of print, as publishers come and go, so I've pieced together a sequence of poems that have proven popular over the years.

Choosing which poems to use in this collection was made easier as my old performance copies of collections fall open readily for the next poem to be aired!

I have also included poems from my 2018 boxed set of poems, *Readings from the Dream Factory*, in order to bridge my past work with my latest poems.

Having ventured into becoming an author, playwright and songwriter, I return to my first writing love: poetry.

I hope you enjoy the collection and hear my voice over the last twenty years of performance and deliberation.

Brendan Hawthorne

# Part One

# Urban Dawn

## Boathouse

A scythe through summer
remarks the buzzing of two-strokes
and the purring of cats
These stretched felines
window-watch work
as they laze on blazing
sun-soaked carpets:
An Eastern frieze
Far away a bell rings
sharp and shrill as a seabird
summoning a flick of the tail
and a twitch of an ear
A curling claw and paw is
followed with yet
another look of complete indifference
Thunder rumbles
on the sand-blasted cobbled quay
as another anthracite rockfall
cracks in the heat whilst
tea is poured
into odd china cups
from a brown-glazed

fat-bellied pot

held stoutly by

a matronly waitress

with boxing glove hands

She hums Londonderry Air

loudly to the world

## High Rise Living (Going Up)

It's hard to keep your feet on the ground
when you're four years old
and seven floors up
Moved from a terrace in '65
on the grounds of 'overcrowding'
That's what the council said
And they made me live with
sixty-seven other families
in a high-rise paradise
which they deemed healthy for children
and not overcrowded
From my window I could see
the other boys and girls
playing on the tarmac
which cracked skulls
and broke bones with ease
I was lucky
I learned to ride a bike in my bedroom
with a fitted carpet and
three-quarter bed to break my fall
When the Tonibell Ice Cream Man chimed
The kids would run to him

like Browning's Piper
dancing and cheering in the summer sun
By the time I got there
money sweating in anticipation
the van would just be leaving
and
as the others slurped through
their Mivvis and their Fabs
I got the smell of spent gas
and an eyeful of dust
and then had to make my own way back
alone and empty handed
to ride in the lifts that swam with piss
and then broke down
In my teens I dodged the knives
The television sets
Used nappies and last night's tea
that plummeted from the upper floors
to create pavement art
And sometimes – sadly
it rained cats and dogs
The janitorial sterility was exchanged for filth
They stole your gas meters when you were out
and the hi-fi
Someone's architectural dream

had become my nightmare
though
through years of experience
I managed to catch the Tonibell calf
and return in triumph
with a blue bubblegum Screwball

## Exhibition

We carved silhouettes
from the wings of moths and butterflies
carefully mounting the depictions
of murder and suicide upon
bright steel pins
A display of transience
Transience
in all its abstract
and perfunctory disguises
We filed images in airless
black-framed vaults
encapsulating the moment
killing off tomorrow's sunrise
for fear of making further mistakes

## Industrial Nation

Corrosion creeps along acid-rain rivers
that fume through the streets of life
impregnating decay
with rigidity and fragility
Ferric nightmare atrocities
span astro-cities
shooting holes through plate steel rims
turning structure into lace-wing butterflies
Crumbled red oxides stain dark earth gorges
The open womb of ore
A maiden made whore
Folk history is played out in song
Stories retold of the region's suffering
at the hands of revolution
progress and profit
Pride is crudely forged
into neo-urbane monuments
traffic island memorials
weeping tears of rust
for diminishing trades
an ill-fitting testament
to those who suffered and died
just trying to survive

## Excursion

The wait is as long as a train
and as empty as an off-peak platform
I watch the litter swirl
Chasing its tail
down a wastepipe whirlpool
of filth and decay
The oversize clock clunks
Cleaves another minute
from my existence and
sends it hurtling down the tracks
and I wait
I wait…
I hear distant echoes calling
Muffled and subdued
A platform rendezvous
giving off all the right signals:
Hugs and kisses
Excited greetings
Sad goodbyes
It is only then when I realise
how far I am away from home
and wonder if my life is really
too far off the rails

## Carrying On

I slept with the phone
that still carried the cadence of your voice

I then ate all of the Love Hearts
that you left me
never once reading the messages
in case they hurt too much

Then I dreamt of nothing
only words
Words and emotions
And
the concept of distance
and its effect on loneliness

## Hotel

How many others
Have rested their heads
Upon this pillow of dreams?
Lied
Cried
And died in someone else's arms
Because anything is better
Than sleeping alone

## Seventies Child

70s child saw films of rocket ships landing on the moon
heard Concorde beating sound overhead
with its slender gooseneck profile
migrating across terraced rooftops and tower blocks

70s child listened to Slade on the eight-track
and could easily recognise a Ford Cortina Mark III
in GLX electric blue from the end of the street
and car crime was depicted with a wire coat hanger aerial

70s child could run for the bus
in patch pocket high-waist Oxford bags
wearing platform sole shoes on pinched feet
and tank tops over penny round picture shirts

70s child was fed on beef dripping
meat and two veg main courses and suet dumpling desserts
and saw the world through Vesta packet meals
by just adding water and simmering for twenty minutes…

70s child took risks on no brake wrecks
Ate in fast food and Horlicks burger joints
Had conversation other than game boxes and mobile

phones

and didn't know what a designer label meant

70s child could ride on free-flowing motorways

and funked-up wide handlebar Chopper bikes

before going through a string of world crises

Ban the Bomb protests and other boom-bust projects

70s child survived power cuts, pay cuts and Muhammad Ali uppercuts

and pogoed into punk with a trendy leftover feather cut

then waved flags in time to God Save The Queen

and witnessed democracy from the end of a dole queue

70s child is now sipping a pretentious little Chardonnay

A cappuccino from a refurbished dockside café

and contemplates the blameless society over an expanding waistline

and wonders where the bloody hell it all went wrong!

## She Walks at Midnight

Moonless midnight water
Ink-black and oil-slack
engulfs porcelain skin
in breakwater terminations

Her skirt is puckered tight
into the waistband
framing shapely legs
pale and smooth

Cold saline nips at toes
as cruisers glide by
She is lost to the light
and deep in oceans of thought

She is a fragile fragrant flower
carelessly tossed overboard
waiting to be found amongst
broken shells and scattered driftwood
that litter the shoreline
with sadness and hope.

## In Her Arms I Awake

breathing in

out

in out

in

rise and fall

fall and rise

so much easier

to synchronise

than taking turns

when cast upon

lunar tides

where crayfish keepers of dreams reside

ascending from depths

of sub-conscious memory

to lift us gently

on mind-swell seas

that rise and fall

fall and rise

breathing in

out in

out

in

## The Passing of Days

The whole room smells of old pianos and chiming clocks
Of afternoon tea
Salmon and cucumber sandwiches
Starched tablecloths and pipe smoke
Cutlery ringing out togetherness
Hands breaking bread with family
Hosting parties of well-being and laughter
They were in love to the end
She sits by the window now
Gazing out in long shifts
Waiting in hope to hear his boots
once more upon the sandstone step
It was his long shifts that separated them then
just as they do now
His hard-bitten hickory pipe
burns cold these days
And the craze-cracked
old leather tobacco pouch is as dry as his cough
She turns to smooth out the cushions
on his orthopaedic chair

They have a habit of looking like he has just stood up
and gone to fetch a paper from down the road
She looks around to their shelf-full of memories
before laying the table for two
just in case she's wrong

## Love on a Grand Scale

If I could paint a corner of sky
and hang it on a moment
it would be here and now

I would paint it from the finest blue
and embellish it with gold
so you could see the rising sun
and I could watch it set

One day we shall part
and then meet again to share
another day in each other's arms
so when that day closes
we shall count the stars as they shine
happy in our memories

Just two soul mates
never to be apart
under a canopy of sky

# Part Two

# Slide

## Subliminal Effect

Snow is falling as soft as cats' paws
drifting into featherbed slumbers
Ruckled in unease as it awaits the rain
to bring on premature thaws from
rolling clouds that glimly masquerade an opal moon
And I await the midnight spectres
that tarry on the stair-well during sunlight hours
migrating north when light wears thin
to come knocking at my door
knowing it's a double-lock double-barrel
keeper at the gates that hinders them
But if they're patient they will find the keys to my attic
or wear down my resistance in time
They know how to haunt my mind
training my dreams before
riding them full tilt into nightmares
and head on into flurries of madness
as snow falls
as soft as cats' paws
drifting

## Prediction

An acid drop sun descends beneath
the parasol of the eastern seaboard horizon
melanomically corroding the skin
condensing erosion into the Parma Violet scent
so prevalent in your raven wing hair.
As I kiss you, the headiness of your perfume
lies decadently upon my tongue
Invading my senses as clouds stretch
along the bay in evening easy chair repose
They can do no more to stop
the stars igniting one by one
in your midnight curfew eyes
and I see those dark angels
burning on seasoned crosses
projecting cruciform stills
from the back of your mind
as I wonder what fate lies in wait for me.

## Promises

I lie cruciform
set against
the carpet of night
where clouds
slip behind stars
in veiled processions
Driven on
by savage winds
they melt the sails
of tall ships
exposing the wounds
of passengers
to the elements
Blood flows
A liquid fire
on the horizon
laps on the banks
of existence
breaking through
glass barriers
breaking in
breaking out
fighting the bitter ill
with one more

sweetened swill
in this rat-run
run-along
of time
And I wait
You wait
We wait
for that wave
to rip through
our maze
of confusion

## Desert Rose

This desert moulds
dry riverbed pavements
into serpentine sidewinders
grey as snakes and
as cracked as bones

Between neon facades
and fast food-to-go oases
midnight fires blaze
along flaring freeways
in grain-of-sand testimony
to the speed of life
and the epoch of existence

But this thin-skinned entity has
no orange blossom
to fragrance its breath
No will to temper
the sulphurous
twilight chiller winds
that chase pollution plumes
across jaundiced skies

Beneath the yellow stars
of sodium enclosures
tumbleweed container-spoils
haunt empty parking bays
residue from
throw-away take-aways
and midnight copulations

Road-sweepers gather their charge
as solar strobe
rapid-pulse xenon beacons
illuminate the
doorway face of a man
with the peel and smile
of a salamander

He spits on the ground
before ordering a
set meal for one
as a single rose falls
from a forgotten table
left waiting in a wilderness
where love lies deserted

## I Know I've Had Enough

I know I've had enough single malt
when I start seeing doubles
An optical illusion
sells me moss and peat
not heather and thistle
That amber sap sparkles
in crystal decanters
and plays the ancestral pipes
in my head: how I weep
bitter melancholic tears
into my cut glass
The room spins uncontrollably
as I wait for the music to stop
My mouth is no longer
the right shape for words
it opens and closes
without cohesion
The world is now
one step ahead
as I find bottle and glass
lying empty

I am now incapable of lies
I love everyone
with absolute compassion
The women all look younger and prettier
than they did an hour ago
and if they play their cards right
they can have their drunken prize
They can watch me
snore myself to sleep
noise as loud as a jet engine
with dribble oozing from the corner of my mouth
onto freshly ironed lace pillowcases
That'll be the only damp patch
I'll be capable of tonight
until breakfast guts the stomach
and with a rub of the stubble
and a scratch of the arse
the search will be on
for another bottle
of Ireland's finest
to freshen my breath
and I can regain my hold
on alcoholism.

## Caravan Site Blues

Rain rattles tin can alley
Rhythmically beating out
Its random report
Diving earthbound
Unannounced
And craving attention
Soaking into rainhoods
Permeating bobbing
Waterproofs as bright
As fishing floats
Diving into backwaters
Coursing along gutters
And steaming in cars
Turning the air cerulean
Awaiting the respite
Of key in the door relief
And whistling kettles
Excited by the odour
And roar of
Blue is the Colour of Calor
Romance flutters
A sodden butterfly
Airing its wings
Sending shiver fingers

Down the spine

As we hold each other

In this moment

Praying for more rain

## Ghost Train

Fairground rockets and gondolas
lie half buried in shady ditches
next to gilded pipe organs and oversized
multi-coloured clothes and shoes
Barley twist horses no longer
get around to the fun of the fair or
career carelessly towards carefree
wind-in-the-mane heights of dizzy
excitement and nausea
Big dipper tunes once waltzed
the night and day away
barring the rolling eyes of one-armed bandits
from penny play promise arcades
lucky strike golden nuggets
and fruit bowls of racked up fortunes
their lights extinguished forever as
gaudy paint dulls through a combination
of poor maintenance and the mist of melancholia
The gloss is matting with modernity
and laughter once as nimble as candy floss fades
on the turn of years like old photographs
parading tears, smiles and grimaces

from the ‘do-we-have-to?’ situations
and ‘come-on-it’ll-be-fun’ dares.
And how I wish I could trade a day now
to return to that field and feel the wind
from big wheel revolutions
on my youthful face instead of hearing
dry leather limbs creak
grey with age and cynicism
Even the destiny card automaton
sees that it has no future
Yet as these images fall from my eyes
into life experience keepsake boxes
a horn honks in the distance
and the made-up face of a clown
relishes the last laugh on
the remaining member of his audience
before taking his place
in the mausoleum of innocence
and I smile at the fact of once knowing him

## Fantasy for Two

Across starlit pavements
we'd run
Feet echoing
in electrical
fallout stammerings
stored up from
the last storm
that swept over our faces
leaving tears to dry
at each other's fingertips
We slipped between
words of prophecy
guilt and passion
searching for
each other's arms
each other's mouths
intensity building
to the beat
of hearts and streets
driving passion
like the rain

that fell

as we waited

impatiently

for our next breath

to deliver us

from the realms

of fantasy

## Crucible

I think that the sea
must be
made up of
broken cars
that have careered
off the ring road

their diamond filter
headlamps
jamming up
in a relentless wave
sequence
grinding away
at the hardcore

temperature remaining
as steel-cold as
touchstone mercury:
evasive
uncaring
unrelenting

wave

upon wave

crash

upon crash

in need of a holiday

before a breakdown

## Eternal

Each morning
I will gather stars
for you
and place them
in our basket of dreams
so that I can
see them reflect
in your smiles
and in your eyes
I will then collect
the sunlight
that falls on
brightly coloured flowers
and give it to you
so that when it rains
we'll see rainbows
and clouds
will melt away
because of
our happiness
in being together
And when night falls
I will let in

the moonlight
so that we can sleep
peacefully
wrapped
in our love
for each other
until morning
when I will
gather the stars
and place them
in our basket of dreams
for you
for all time
simply
because I love you

## Thoughts From The Café Terrace At Arles By Night 1888

### (Inspired by Vincent Van Gogh)

Stars fall in sulphur blooms

sweet-scented desert roses

Moroccan moonshine

clatters silver trays

serving coffee and Absinthe

Waiters see all

and say nothing

They smile through

black topiary moustaches

accenting the night

with fashion

Cobbled streets ribble

with reflections

of shop window lights

Illuminated stained glass

projections of complex

woven threads

embroider

cosmopolitan colours

on the clothes of
painted socialites
who chatter nonchalantly
with tomb-raiders and
body-snatchers
where poets and artists
freeze-dry images
of sinuous nouveau nights
through steaming beverages
and the scent
of sweet warm cognac
This temple of light
draws crowds
like moths towards incandescence
They settle
They deal
They drink
Before walking home
anonymously into the night
richer for the trip

## Stratagem

she breathes fire
through
cinnamon fingers

her dark eyes
shut tight

he sucks
on ice
from the glass

curling his toes
like sticklebacks

their last words
edged in gilt
intimately reflecting

that their
war is over

and they were
missing it already

# Part Three

# The All Night Café and Other Dives

## Snooker Hall Queues

Crazy gets the snorts from onlookers
through the cellar gloom for his
double-over fluke off the baulk
The old back hand trick-shot
perfected with the promise of
crisis money riding on the cushion
Seems to have spent his life
at the end of a cue
fighting off the constipation of losing
Leaving all that to the opposition
who suffer from piles for sitting too long
on cold benches in draughty passageways
where the air clings like peaches in syrup
and waistcoat pockets sag
like beer bellies from the weight of
Superking filters and scuffed blue chalk cubes
drilled with concentrated precision
on cork tip reamers in the run up
to 'winner stays on' game rules
Floodlit ivorine clacks and
buffets the leather before sinking
below the moss green baize

waiting for the numbers to play out
chasing the colours in high break
snowballs on the side
Brass markers nudge along scoreboards
their bows edging ever closer
to the flattened pint of victory
Feet stick to floors
like flies to the ceiling
and honeytraps snap as giggly supporters
receive a jack-the-lad smile and a wink
as he kisses the pink and eyes up the mini skirts
lined up on stools waiting to welcome him home
as he steadies the readiness
for the seven black
to reap its rewards

## The So Long Saloon

Lipstick gin and shandy cocktails
are poured in front of the misted mirror
for especially chosen clientele
where spittoons rim shot ring
with extra strength ricochets
and sawdust chokes the cockroaches
during Cucaracha step encores
Last round fights
punch out the lights
before cold damp streets
swallow up the swagger
But the rush to the bar is slow
and paying is as distasteful
as the thoughts of the last
pole dancer of the evening
when thinking of those
who have publicly ground themselves
into the apparatus
before them
Under the flickering tar-coated
flycatcher tubes that dimly
illuminate the rattling skittle alley

and knocking domino stadia
is where they gather
Those with puckered up pumped up lips
that suck down throw back whiskey chasers
making speaking uneasy
in the snug and the smoke
The sandwich bell rings
and pies and cobs let out a stale stench
as sour as old Tom's whiskers
and with just as much meat
as he sits in his overcoat
picking out the hairs
from flake pork scratchings
Chewing on his gums
he congratulates himself
on how some things
will simply never change

## Ballroom Etiquette

Smiles fixed with hairspray and gel
are all set for the performance of painted
mannequins crafted with the intent
of Pinocchio's puppet master parent
Another chip falls from a paper plate
into the shag pile
before a routine of Latin A
stretches patent leather and Lycra
to the limits - as they beat the competition
to the turns using raised elbow bumpers
and 'kill you in a moment' stares.
Then there's a tease towards the judges
to shade a point with a pout and a point
with a thrust and a skinny shimmy shaker
money maker cha cha cha
Hot heats are in strict double time
ready to melt each waxen face moulded
from determination and tears of
'not good enough' realisation
Stages flash by in spotlight intensity
blurring ringside plastic palm trees
cocktail lounges and toupees

into a stereo syncopated pastiche
And before you know it
it's the waltz before bedtime
where shuffles are sent groping
into the drizzle-drunk
rain-stained night air
where the back seat of a Ford Capri
beckons a few moments of intimacy
somewhere on a shadowy car park
left unattended from ten

## Downstairs At Mikey's

Anaemic light leeches through
polluted basement windows
Stricken faces are heavy and sullen
all blue lipped and mean
An overcoated in-crowd sits
hypnotically carving their names
into beer-soaked tabletops
and dimly lit corners are
inhabited by poets and chin scratchers
frowning at their free coffee refills
stewed beyond any flavour of
dark roast Americana Arabica
freeze dried on commercial fair-trade winds
to avoid the complexity of guilt
They engorge their blistered minds
on purple amaretti biscuits
and spirit lamp warmed brandy
Wantonly they tear pages from dog-eared notebooks
only to leave them lying naked and
scattered across sugar-coated
ring-marked mock mahogany fittings
Knotted fingers with hard-bitten nails

caress the handwritten words
now seen as something to be loathed
and something to be suspicious of:
priming them with paranoid stinging venom
to set barbed wire snares with which
to torment innocent eyes with chosen truth
Concepts are scattered
to the prevailing winds
of generational trends
as streetwise counterfeits
await news on the quiet revolution
chatting undercover
with flash bomb paparazzi sniffers
whilst pens lie bleeding
downstairs at Mikey's:
the place where non-believers
dine out on fatal abstractions

## Scrapyard Finality

brazier bonfires
smoke apocalyptically
across axles
shells
and sky scrapper towers:
the end of the road
for failures
and break down tow-ins

family tourers
and sporting coupes
line up
wing mirror to wing mirror
retired from service
given mortuary mentality
in a rainbow of finishes
for oxyacetylene torches
to splutter scalpel wrecks
into donor consumables
for the scavengers
to feast their eyes

and wallets upon

at the gate
a portacabin with caravan
extension sales office
houses the spoils
where coffee
as thick as sump oil
is given freely to regulars
to drink beside
the strained chain
'I dine here'
guard dog
as he watches over
transmission transactions
that turn Monday moans
into Sunday pride
and dried up dinners

# Part Four

# Readings from the Dream Factory

## What Shape the Poet's Gravestone?

### (Dream at Sylvia Plath's graveside Nov 14, 2014 - dusk)

Should it
iconically reach out to stars, moon and cosmos?
Draw an audience on cadence?
Should it be planted deeply into the Earth's vibrant core?
Its sweet head resting like daisies in spring
Should it be marble? Granite?
Should it curl like smoke or cloud
Wind-blown on tomorrow's muse
or carved gently in rippling waves?
Or beset rolling like a fretted grey sea?
Should angels take flights of fancy
or stand solemnly with praying hands?
Should they hold the open arms of the cross
or should it be just plain and simple?
A tablet with a name and profession
Should all words and dust be cast to the elements
and left omnipresent in the ether
for those who knew them once
re-embodied to gather in garlands of memory
as we sit lovingly here
at this final resting place
of a soul once troubled?

## Wolf

### (A dream on a train to London)

I feast upon your lips
as they part
in bouts
of slumber pouts
Latent passion
Stretches
Entrapment
spittle webs
from
upper
to lower side
lip-gloss
Your shadowed eyes
remain closed
through shuttered
fluttered R.E.M. spasms
Your thighs part
in relaxed awareness
as you play out
your particular brand of fantasy
close to your heart

On awakening
your ecstatic sighs of
sub-consciousness
climax in
gasps of breathless longing
before you return
to that place
I want to join you there
Behind your eyes
where no one can see us
running naked
towards the dimpled hollow
of satiety:
A place
where we can howl at the moon
completely undisturbed

## Dreamtime

### (A dream in Binham, Norfolk)

Summer hums on languid air
where irises dip
artistic fingers
into the sparkling palette
of a lazy stream
Wheat fields ripple
in ripening sunshine
and wistful
wayside blooms
nod reclining heads
in soporific breezes
that send my mind
towards the realms of sleep
Light-as-a-feather-bed birds
glide thermals
for leisure and the kill
whilst the idle
noisily
migrate in swift-shaped
jet stream airliners
across a scarred sky-blue sky

From their cocooned vantage point
they see
hear
and feel so little of today
And I wonder if they will ever
find something of themselves
upon reaching that far flung destination
when all that they had to do
was sit with me and dream
on a day
a simple day when
summer hums its tune

## Last Night We Danced

### (A dream of the Tower Ballroom)

There were no barriers
to intimacy
or ability
and we only had eyes
for each other
as we caressed
the floor with our
snuffed leather soles
Holding each other
in posed-for determination
we were sent on a crazed
fairground ride
spinning
pirouetting
and fish-tailing
between tables bedecked
with beacons of kinetic romance
Each candle flame
a power-point
drawing desires
and igniting fantasies
as imaginations

chased mirage images
of fleeting shadows
to the walls
as they filed
through the
simmering haze
of soft eye focus
and distant gaze
each in turn presenting
another world
to our panting
physicality
And last night
we danced
beneath a
glitter ball moon
as it spun silently under
a ceiling of stars

## Calle Muros Mijas

### (A dream at Mijas, Spain)

Snow blind white walls
sidelined with the
potted balconies
of Mijas they
blare clarions sharp as church bells
on the spy top vistas
of burnt earth
refracted through
stained glass bulls' eyes
the colours of donkey braids
The gaze extends
towards jasmine beds
'ahhhhing'
heady intentions
beneath the shimmering ripple roof tiles of
terracotta sun dried half pipes
now resembling the
bare spines of gecko backs
blistering to the rhythm
of cicadas along the Calle where
bleached sweated lace
stained in silhouette
leans in shade against la Alcazaba doorway

She licks exotic flavours
from her dry pout lips
where honey drips
from sweat black hair
tossed in serious sensuality on
breezes
that are now
lazy in heat
heavy in tradition
bent on antiquity
charged with excitement
And today I sensed it all
to absolute satiety

## Playtime

### (A dream at Wednesbury)

At dusk
she paddles
in newly formed
pavement puddles
Shaking mercurial beads
from silver dancing slippers
she captures slivers
of moonshine
in the rippled splashes
of playtime
Her laughter is
as light as a breeze
chasing remnant clouds
to a distant horizon now
revealing star shine
pinpoints
one-by-one
from their distant worlds
She looks askance
and scowls
at an intrusive
sitting room light

that pierces curtains
from across the street
dulling the sparkle
for a moment
as she recognises herself
in a frozen reflection
Time had been forgotten
through playtime indulgences
She hadn't heard her
Mommy calling and so
she recoils at
how quickly those
sixty years
have simply passed her by

# Part Five

# Sixty Something...

## The Order of Words

I was born with the devil's hand
Held in Christian righteousness
and educated in the progressive sixties
where right-handed scissors
cut jagged lines
and my writing spelt s d r a w k c a b
across the feint ruled pages
searching for the secure margins
of left handedness
A caggy
A leftie
That was me
They told my mom I'd be disadvantaged
They told my mom they hit me with rulers
to break the creative spirit
get my measure and
take me out of my right mind
Readied to conform to the British standards
of an intolerant and blinkered society
My creative side was red taped down
by bureaucratic fools
My written communication suffered
My art suffered
I became mirrored in vision:

Barricaded
Closed down
Shuttered up
My good *bad* hand tied behind me
left only to throw salt
to blind the demon's eye
whilst experts comforted me
with earnest patronising precision
telling me I'd be better off
when I was right…
And the frustration grew
And the barriers built
And intelligence could not find
a way through the tangled webs
of institutionalised confusion
Letters formed but sentences
couldn't flow at the rate
of an untamed mind
where imagination knew no bounds
I remained shackled
because they said so
I fluffed exams
because I didn't comprehend
I mixed sentences like the lifetime one
those educationalists gave me
I drifted to find escape routes

I tried to dig my way out
but ‘b’s were ‘d’s and algebra
was purely x-rated
So they taught me French instead
as if my problems weren’t acutely accented enough

## I Always Wondered

I always wondered why he stared at the ground
when there was so much to look at all around

Like cooling towers and demolition sites
boarded up shops and high-rise flats
and silent factories with seeping outfall
choking Jack Bannocks in the canal

I always wondered why he stared at the ground
when there was so much to look at all around

Like burned out cars and derelict scrapyards
Smoke stack sunshine igniting box crane sunsets
burning holes in dog walk photos

I always wondered why he stared at the ground
So I asked him why and he said

that he wasn't staring at the ground
In fact he was looking in puddles with oilskin sheens
that reminded him of furnace limestone cobbles

And that on reflection the sky passes you by
and that you don't get a crick in your neck
from looking around all day long when
all you are doing is waiting for rain

## Lost Youth

It was just there
where we turned left
Or was it right?
When we went
round the traffic island
for the third time
The one with
the cones
The cones
that have become a landmark
in their own right
A memorial to temporary permanence
Remember when
I said that's where it was?
The pub I bought my first pint in
when I was sixteen
The acne and bum fluff gave me away
but they still served me
even if I did vomit off the top step
of the lounge where the drinks were dearer
It must be about where that oil drum is
next to the poppy by the wall
and the burned-out scooter
Yes that's it just there

The pool table was where
that puddle is now
I remember the bost off
that nearly took
the head off the landlord
as red ball cannoned off middle pocket
with a screwed spin
that raised it above the baulk
and ricocheted off the serving hatch
All the landlord had wanted to know was
if we were 'ok for drinks?'
He went as pale as his apron...
But how we laughed
We got wasted on this building site
at twelve pence a pint
and ten pence on the cush.
The juke box was always playing Dixie
I think it was double-four time
We were all in dire straits then
And now it's gone
But that's where it was
Just there
where we turned right
or was it left?

## J, Carl and Me

On Saturdays
we'd meet at J's
7.30 to 8 a.m.
Pocket money
to wages
To spend as we pleased
on old stuff
or a new release
J's mom would
fill our bellies
with doorstep
bacon sandwiches
and steaming
mugs of tea
Us three:
J, Carl and me
Off we hopped
by train to Brum
buying records until
we dropped
And it was back to J's

music-only front parlour
where we'd play our songs
through excess volume
And pretty soon
The Marquee Moon
punctuated the prog
and Donna's disco moan
We'd take intervals of tea
and fill up on
Victoria Sponge
And how we'd laugh
and J would dance
and sing odd lyrics
to any old song
if he was given
half a chance
And remember that day
on Dave's diamond
crazy lead break
'Dum dum dum dum derrrr'
the tiles fell off the grate
and we spent many an hour
piecing them all back together

with no help from Joan in Personnel
In time
we went our own ways
and lost touch
as you do
over the days
that turn into years
When now became
tomorrow afternoon
Carl told me that
J had passed away
to many rolling tears
But then
I heard a favourite song
to sing along because
memories you'll find
are never that far behind
They are here
as fresh as today
and in my mind
J's mom still feeds us
plates of butties
and the turntable

plays something new from J
fresh from the days
when we all
had something to say
Because somewhere
out there
J still plays his songs
and laughs
as he dances and sings
now he's free to be
who he wanted to be
And there's music
lined up once again
Just one more platter
for J
Carl and me

## Timeless Shores

### (Inspired by a photograph by Jon Watkiss)

Grounded wings
Of ocean flight
Caress sharp shingle
In dawn's first light

From distant waves
As grey as sky
The shutter opens
On the camera's eye

Captured sunlight
Penetrates night
Invading space
Once lost to sight

Let Venus sleep
Beyond the moon:
Two crescent halves
Made whole soon

A scene laid bare
Upon bedrock creation
A freeze frame grist
Of brine-baked migration

The gull descends
To the curlew's cry
The yawning shell
Serves passers by

With nature's whys
And all its wherefores
Tides will return to
Timeless shores

## Reluctance

I don't want to live here anymore:
I feel trapped
Imprisoned
Contained

I am claustrophobic:
Panic ridden
Tearful
Frustrated

I could live by sea
Find out what it is to be me
Contemplate the sunshine and
its effects on vitamin D

Would I be complete though
without the people I love?
Without my LPs!
All the people I know?

I could live in the mountains
Feel the heat of the day
and the cold of the night
Be reborn when feeling old

Breathe air
that doesn't shred my lungs
with chemical overload
But would I feel complete
with no guitars?

I could live by a stream
Drop out
Cop out
without a care

Watch clouds all day
Feel the seasons
Witness
birth and decay

No mobile phone
No computer
Just observing
ebb and flow
But would I be complete
without TV?

I could live by myself
remove my mardiness
from those around me
Those I care for

Be left to my own devices
Become my own worst enemy
Store up words and emotions
Get plenty to say with no one to listen

But none of this would be complete
without an audience
and so I think it best
to sensibly stay where I am
and simply take          another          deep          breath

## Midnight Kites

Midnight kites
strain at the leash
Tightening cords
held brittle cold
on midnight air
Marching and stamping
we pirouette in hold
held in tenuous
embrace
Diamond cartouche tails
wave on sidereal tides
adjusting tension
upon the full face
phase of kinetic lunacy
Colours are muted
Painted for the sun but in reflection they
are low light pale
carrying dreams and
heaven-bound prayers
made of earthly card
and string from Woolworths
They struggle to be free
Fighting the onrush push
towards infinite truth

## Mind Blown

In my mind is an ocean
of blue:
Of cobalt
sapphire and
azure
sent spinning
in whirlpool tones
and hues
as vast and as deep
as anything you can imagine
Sometimes the waters are calm:
lazy and tranquil
warm and basking beneath
internal skies
of filtered sunlight
Other times the moon
awakens my dreams
removes them
from rearing cray fish claws
along the banks of the silver river
lit on the mirrored surface
with Milky Way lustre
When the tide changes
and mind breezes

turn to storm force
the rolling waves
of nightmares
dredge the past
from hidden depths
to veneered surface
Do not be shocked
Do not be afraid
if demons and ghosts
flash across my
light spangled face
For if you truly know me
you know it is not me
It is *of* me
And when waters are troubled
and you abandon me like
a man overboard
don't think you can
return to be at my side
the next time the sun shines
My true friends
swim with me now:
Ride storms and cut new wakes
Together
on our next encroaching tide

## Glass Swans

You'd see 'em
Graduated glass swans
looking like ducks in a row
Paddling in clear glass
across white lead gloss paint
in the windows
of terraced front bays
Up and down the street
they'd migrate
Big 'uns
Little 'uns
All with a cooled curve
pinched bill head and
swept with a flourish
that only skill can promote
in a single flick
At the tamp down
ashtray space between
bulbous wings
the base was
nipped and sheared
and stretched
into a majestic arch

fine and fragile
They all wanted them
Neighbours clamoured for end-of-day artistry
Treasures to ornament
the sparse shelf
that allus faced out to passers by
never into the room
for the occupants to admire or look over
On a rainy day it was
something to trap the sun
In summer
from factory darkness
the swans reminded us
of those who
sweated and toiled
Wore the grime on their backs
manufacturing grace and beauty
from the noise and dust
and the heat from hell
Things that only a gift shop
could truly afford
When the shift ended
the spoils were shared
simply with a homeward journey
knock on the door and
a reach into an overcoat

Another swan produced
'This one for the mantle Mrs Turley?'
'No. It'll look good in the bay
Facing out towards them over the road'

## Old School New Desk

We sat side by side
A lift up desk
under which to hide
Ten bob to keep out
This one's mine
I'd pull Bev's pony tail
when she was
reading the board

I was the loner
I lived in angry silence
Frustration boiled over
I kicked the teacher
who told my mom
I'd be alright when I was older
And now the desk stands empty:
free from the noise and clatter
and the nitter natter chatter

I remember the rock hard
inherited chewing gum
so from sheer boredom
I hewed tasteless Bazooka Joes
that clung in rock cakes
to the underside of the desk
They scraped your legs

when you fidgeted
We kept our pencil shavings
in the inkwells
and redundant ceramic pens
with copper nibs
in the cupboard

We were all victims of the biro
once you'd mastered the pencil
The brass slide that covered the dried up wells
were glued shut with PVA
so the ink monitors lost a job
under health and safety regulations
in a vain attempt
to save trapped fingers

But you could still shut your head
In the desk or
give yourself an uppercut
when the lid jammed
due to overrun shangers
of heavy yacht varnish
the caretaker applied when facilities closed
for the six weeks summer hols

We never sailed anywhere
Only in daydreams
Those ink bloom stains
were circled by compass point pock marks

and inane scratched on graffiti
I didn't know Julie let alone love her
And just whose is this left over sock
left festering at the back?

On the upside there's a spelling test
with answers
(unfortunately more wrong than right)
And Tracey kept a stash of transfers
to put on our arms
She fixed them with milk
and covered them with aluminium bottle tops
And Lavinia was sent to a special school
because she wore jelly sandals

But I have to admit
as I carved my initials and stated
that I was there
that I did like T. Rex and quite fancied Cher

## Heart Shadow

There is an eclipse
taking place
deep within his being
found radiating through his soul
From the space that stored love
emerges a creeping shadow:
A red giant
preparing to outgrow itself
expanding by degrees
it is running out of fuel
Walls are collapsing
under their own pressure
It is no longer possible
to surf the sinuous sinewave
that is now
out of time and kilter
with the pulsating prism
The bleep of life
is out of phase
with itself and the machinery
They said he had a big heart
Here's the X-ray to prove it
Look! Before the beat stops
and the rhythm ceases

## Patchwork Days

The sky is the colour of denim
Patched up with fair weather puffballs
drifting lazily on thermals of intent
Trees beckon breezes
through outstretched limbs
delivering change wherever
it may find itself
to further gather its thoughts
into future deluges of creativity
for the freewheel mind
Aviators of all kinds scar
the scene with vapour trails of escapism
A place where birds prove
they are miles ahead
in the evolution of flight
Silhouettes dance across my vision
in and out of shade
as shadows of strangers
become transient to light
And on awakening from my dream
I connect with reality
Raising up I see the shoes
that have walked many earthbound miles
and my jeans are the colour of sky
and talk incessantly of patchwork days

## Twilight

Sunset trees are restless now as
solar winds draw them home
to landscape rest
A party balloon moon is rising steeply
against deepening reddening skies
as stars gain presence in magnitude
and planets parade their worlds:
systems of co-existence
waltzing in timed romance
And in this verdant twilight
thick with honeysuckle scent
I see the universe in an instant
as my world goes rushing by
Blackbirds call before bedtime
upon the evening lull
as insects make the last run home
to warm their hollow hive
A helicopter scythes through siren ambiance
as another chase-down on urban life
is performed in a place
where night time rarely falls
but nature retains its calls
And if it wasn't for domestication
we would still live on the edge

where life and death are a sigh apart
balanced upon an urban village ledge
We are seekers demanding deliverance
from an all-encroaching emptiness
as treelines disappear for good
under the Jack Boot of
so called progress

## Unremarkable

I didn't pay much attention to the lady
sitting cross legged on the tarmac
in car park bay 47
Her rainbow bag
bangles, beads and ankle bells
were all ringing in her new age
But I didn't pay much attention to her
She faced the setting twilight
which softened her face
as she posed in salutation to the sun
But I really didn't notice her
If she held her right arm out
she could touch the tidal mark of bay 46
and by letting her left arm float
she could fingertip touch bay 48
But I barely noticed the lady as her
years gave way
To tie dye acid etched cheesecloth
terminating in string sandals
sign posting painted nails
beautifully presented on long straight toes
Neither did I take much notice as
her alpha rhythms sync'd to divinity
and connected with multi-plane

crystal pyramids and other interdimensional portals
I suppose she was airing her past lives
I wonder if she'll remember this car park in the future?
I didn't pay much attention to her though
Really not at all
Maybe I should have said 'hello'?

## Pub Wake

Steel penny shutters
weigh down screwed lids
on old pub faces
Their features tired and drawn
Grimly tattooed with acid tags
etched into crafted masonry
Time is called
Last drinks are swallowed
and levelled before the brickwork
Glasses are left where they fall
Crystallised foam left to stain
the walls of trading standard pint glasses
before bedtime calls
No-one wants to stare at those tar coated walls anymore
Pick at spiral patterned anaglypta
that is dimly lit in mock Victorian romance
Tacky tables are stacked with vacant chairs
No names are left
except in the diddlum book
filed at the back of the dartboard
There will be no more after factory hours get togethers
or sing songs from the regulars
No more sniffing the barmaid's apron
or seeing goggle-eyed beauty through a narcotic fug

No more stale beer to add sticky
to the already sticky carpet
that's so far gone it smells like sick
And where the hell will we go
when the last traditional pub is laid to rest?
Where would we hold the wake
when they're each and every one
dead and gone?

## Factory Waste Ground

Behind the grey mossed up asbestos sheds
that stand in corrugated wavelets
there was a waste ground
Footprints of old brick outbuildings
lie in silent testament
to more industrial times
Obsolete in retirement
But on this waste ground
grew a multitude of wildflowers
from the palest acrid yellows
to furnace reds and cold morning blues:
From a hint of pink to purple hues
a real rag bag production
of styles and designs
and every summer it buzzed with insects
and scurrying wildlife
prey birds circled
and butterflies fluttered in manic zigzags
This tranquility was shattered
when the 7.30 a.m. Bullhorn Klaxon
started up the gennys
and the hammering and the welding
until the knock-off cacophony ceased
and the day wound down

But the waste ground became a meadow:
A pre-shift meditation
A break time haven
and a finishing time detox
When winter's veil cleared away
summer's calicoes
the foxes would bring their cubs
to the old boys who shared their sandwiches
and gently rescued birds caught in
mathematical girderwork
Now that humanity that once clung to industry
has gone
The waste ground-turned-meadow
that clung to the grey asbestos wall
has been lost
The factory gates closed
for a housing estate to open
on scrubbed soil
with concrete drives and paved patios
all in the name of habitation corridors
political spite
and investment opportunities

## Sleepwalking

How many times have I kissed you
whilst you sleep?
As softly as a summer's breeze
that caresses your lips
as they silently hold the secrets
I hear that you keep

How many times have I held you
whilst you sleep?
As gently as if you were finest porcelain
that would simply crumble
under the pressure of time's fingers
as they slowly creep

How many times have I said sorry
whilst you sleep?
Whispered in case I awoke you
from dreams that clearly engage you
And how I wished it could be different
if you could only hear my heart weep

How many times have I left you
whilst you sleep?
Deserted you through the onslaught
of my own rampaging fears
and wished that if you could hold me
we could have changed the harvest
we both now reap

## Remember Me?

Remember me?
I am an eight-track play back
magnetic head of drawn-in opposing natures
A fuzz tone memory bank
in a valve-lit mind sparking up
Igniting the darkest
recesses of a hardwired mind
Ready to take on board and
regurgitate from chrome dream reel laminates
Press play
Press rewind
Press fast forward
But never hit delete
When I rest my head
at sunset and close my eyes
I know I will have done
all that I could
Said all things that needed to be said
Sung my own song
and listened to yours
But for now I will carry on –
it being the nature of things
I embrace the soul born spirit
unencumbered by physicality

A gentle breath that lasts an eternity
A light turned low
A song on the radio
A video
A picture
in the photo gallery of time
Replay my memory sometimes
Stop it
Fast Forward >> or rewind <<
But please don't delete me

## The postcard said

'I don't have room
to say much here
other than I'd like to say more
and that if I had the space
I would
and then
I could tell you all about
the caravan park
and the potholes in the dark
and the weather
that remains consistently poor
and the man in the shop
who says he knows you from
when you lived on the estate
He mentioned something
about a blue Lambretta
and a Who ticket?
I told him I'd remind you
But as space
to write
is limited
I won't. So...
Just to say the journey was ok
but the destination

isn't worth it
and that we are making
the best of it
Sister Jodie's sunburn
is only second degree
just like her, eh?
When she moves it's like
shaking a snowdome
Uncle Charlie will be in a cast
for six weeks
following his fall
attempting a desperate toilet run
in the middle of the night
That's how we got to know about the pothole
On the positive side
we think the stain will come out
of his beige holiday slacks
Colin's rash will need time
and an explanation
Jeannie can't remember
where she left her new stilettos
after a night at the social club
but the owner gives her a wink
every time he walks past
so I think he knows something
And the doctor says

the sting
I got on the first night
will go down
once the antibiotics kick in
The waiting room
at the surgery
was nice though
It had your lounge wallpaper
Strange, that!
Really decorative
but I can't say much
for the receptionist
Sorry this is brief
Not much to report on really
so see you next week
upon our return and for now
just to say…
Wish you were here!

Cousin Jim'

## Another Year On

Roller grills grimace
keeping at bay
salt grey sea storms
bent on prising          gaps
between buckets       and       spades
now retired for the winter
They swing violently on faded strings
gaudy gay in summer triumph
ignorant of fickle tourists
and seasonal disinterest
Down the road
arcade lights flash sequentially
to upbeat sixties pop
just in case the bandit revolver barrels
connect with the odds
stacked against the gambler
trying his potbellied luck
There is no Punch and Judy man
There is no audience
except for the birthday boy
with no cake or candles
His wary gaze splits pier planks
to gain vistas on
the heaving grey brine broth

  l l

 o   i

r      n

         g

                  below

Echoes of childhood

resonate between

closed down masonry drill repairs

Where no-one knows it's your day

and no-one cares anyway

because no-one else

is counting the years

but you

## Moths

After the time bell rings
rain falls in
winter slivers
Silver shivers framed
in fireside reflections
as 'one for the road'
last orders serve
flickers of comfort
in a bull's eye glass
whacked down for your daddy o
Bulging road eyes
red with sleep are ready to
set sail on duck down seas
cradling headaches
in crinkled waves
that kiss
the shores of sleep
and all our fitful dreams
can now take flight

## Butterflies in the Rain

Battered, bruised, and war-torn
from airborne tirades
we co-operatively
dissolve in the rain
Fragile wings
draped in exhaustion
our camouflage bleeds
into water colours
into this dry powdered Earth
that crumbles dust-like
beneath our feet
We are stripped
of warning signs
and handy
hideaway tactics
as cloud upon cloud
eclipses our eyes
releasing sweet tears
in deference
to lost innocence
We share the moment:
Spend it
reaching out
as we

drink in the nectar
of sweet words
from the fountains
where tongues
lap loyally
at all truth
Look!
Our garden blooms again
and we are allowed
enough time to
repaint our masks
in preparation
for the new cycle
to commence

## Too Much Night

Passing headlights spin the coving
to the hardboard pelmet rufflette
Don't dazzle, dip!
Design classics:
Vauxhall, Cowley and Morris Garage
roar on choke
in fast-ish getaways
with faceted warning lamps and
speedo dials flickering towards thirty
And now the runaway truck
is bearing down on my dream again
from the fold of the wall
in 90 degrees of sweat
The nights were always claustrophobic
Sometimes whirligig illuminations
became fairground rides
for the kid with no coat
as snow fell on shilling bran tubs
filled with tanner surprises
And the painted horses rode tirelessly along
the gilded Carny tracks of my mind
to the jingle of brassed harnesses
to pipe organ fanfare recitals where
waxen faces melt in the rain

Holiday camp falsehoods
play happy families…
only someone had cut the deck
into razor ribbons of flashbacks
and a paranoid mind became paralysed
by fear from whispers in the corner
where the clown spoke in riddles
before dawn shed light on his dirty face
The painted horse rode me out of town
to the safety of a breakfast table
billowed in yellow gingham
the colour of boiled egg yolks and
lightly buttered toast
neatly cut into diamonds
sickle smiles in shredded marmalade
reminded me of faces in the hallway
only to realise there and then
that the features were mine
and they never left me
I gave them a home in a timeless room
where they haunt me on the dark days
when the sun doesn't rise
in the darkness of a mind
that fears freedom
and hates containment
awaiting the next phobia to call

on the chiming of the clock
where the axe wielding teddy bear
casts his shadow on the wall
and announces the next visitor
to help my nightmares along

## This Brittle Canvas

Geese crease the sky
in broken panes
of factory glass

Their presence shatters
this brittle canvas
into fragments
that cannot sustain changes
by the lazy lob
of marbled furnace bibble
once released from
vandal handedness

Jagged ripples of
frozen in time silvered veins
coagulate in cornered webs
as they form in
over-painted aluminium frames
They capture the image
forming beneath
rust leaks
from cast outfalls
and embossed
rainwater goods

sending old blood leaching
from lost livelihoods
ebbing away into canal basins

Crows fly across
a broken sky
Past the forge's silent throat
as it echoes past glories
in the face of demolition
and a forgotten
redundant trade

## The Artist in Isolation

### (Inspired by a painting by Ian Davies)

In this all but empty room
I am no chameleon
In fact I am easily found
Just there
behind the door
A palette of all that I am
Illuminated stained glass
fragile and framed
If I could hide behind
my own shadow
I would
but its lack of depth precludes
any protective cover
It was you who placed me here
high on this pedestal
but it was me who made
an exhibition of myself
Always wanting to please
Never getting the breaks
Wearing everything
on my outdated
outmoded
calico sleeves

Look at the signs printed in Arial
An easy read font
that commentates on
the clown with tears:
The comic who fears
advancing years
And how I've cried myself to comfort
here in this place of empty
isolation without audience
A back room of indignity
far from the main stage
that once filled me with the light
of my latent creativity
Its absence now denying me
in these unnatural surroundings
I am a display of a bygone day
Out of fashion
Out of platform step
with the world beyond these walls
But I believe that my time will come again
I can do nostalgia
if you ask
Just put a penny in the slot
to pay for my repeats...
But for now
I'll wait in painted silence

with my nightmares of being forgotten
and my dreams of who I really am
in the company of memories
and those who knew me once

# ABOUT THE AUTHOR

Brendan Hawthorne is a poet, playwright, writer and musician, based in the industrial West Midlands. He was first published in 2004 by Bluechrome in the Hobo Poet series, where he was described by a poetry editor and critic as being the 'best Urban Poet of his time.' He has since released four poetry collections through various publishers and seven titles of local interest for Bradwell Books. He writes in both standard English and dialect and celebrates the language and dialect of all sectors of the community.

Over the last twenty years Brendan Hawthorne has grown from a fledgling performance poet into a nationally published author. He is no stranger to the media, either, being a regular on local radio and television and having had appearances on The One Show translating Shirley Bassey lyrics into Black Country dialect to the Dame herself, and a local interest segment on Flog It! He has been interviewed by Adrian Chiles for a BBC documentary and became West Midlands Ambassador for Smooth Radio for a two-year period.

A viral hit in 2017, Brendan's appearance on BBC Radio WM on Black Country Day has gained over a million views to date. Both in 2018 and 2019 Brendan was awarded the Bill o'

Bowes cup for best written dialect award at the National Dialect Festival.

Brendan's work has gone into permanent public art displays and he has also appeared on the fourth plinth in Trafalgar Square as part of Anthony Gormley's art installation where he 'broadcast' work in his much-beloved Black Country dialect.

His community play *Hard Graft: All for Twenty-Three Bob* encouraged those with no stage or singing experience to become part of a sell out performance at Wednesbury Town Hall where all proceeds from ticket sales went to the Mayor's Charity. His more recent radio style WWI play *Two Mothers Of Distant Sons* has also received critical acclaim from audiences. Productions of his plays, poetry and songs have combined his love of storytelling and music.

Throughout those years he has selflessly inspired, encouraged and enabled other writers through workshops, mentoring and facilitating performance spaces to bring spoken word and acoustic music to audiences, culminating in a much-loved and well-attended monthly showcase Ere We Bin.

Brendan was honoured to be made Poet Laureate of Wednesbury in 2014, his adopted home town, and in 2017 was made one of the Black Country 100 Masters. As an arts facilitator, he has worked on numerous commissions including NHS, English Heritage and National Trust.

Brendan is currently an Ambassador for *The Black Country Bugle*.

Find out more or contact Brendan about his work at -

www.brendanhawthorne.org

brendanhawthornepoet61@gmail.com

Photograph courtesy of Lynn P. Hawthorne

# PREVIOUS PUBLICATIONS

***Urban Dawn***

Bluechrome, 2004

ISBN: 1904781853

***Slide***

Poetry Monthly Press, 2007

ISBN: 978906357085

***Exhibit B***

The Kates Hill Press, 2010

ISBN: 9781904552383

***Black Country Dialect***

Bradwell Books, 2013

ISBN: 9781902674513

***Black Country Wit and Humour* (with Camilla Zajac)**

Bradwell Books, 2013

ISBN: 9781902674698

***Ghost Stories of The Black Country and Birmingham***

Bradwell Books, 2013

ISBN: 9781902674704

***Hard Graft: All for Twenty-Three Bob***

Play Script – 2013., The Kate's Hill Press, 2015

ISBN:978-1-904552-48-2

***Warwickshire Dialect***

Bradwell Books, 2014

ISBN:978-1-90991-469-8

***Walks Around the Black Country***

Bradwell Books, 2015

ISBN:978-1-909914-37-7

***Birmingham and Black Country Murder Stories***

Bradwell Books, 2017

ISBN: 978-1910551967

***Readings from the Dream Factory***

Poetry Precinct Press, 2018

***South West Murder Stories***

Bradwell Books, 2018

ISBN:9781912060979

# DREAM WELL WRITING LTD

Dream Well Writing Ltd are Staffordshire based publishers of dyslexia friendly books – with worldwide distribution – and an environmentally conscious ethos.

Find out more about Dream Well at

http://dreamwellwriting.simplesite.com/

https://www.facebook.com/dreamwellwriting/

Printed in Great Britain
by Amazon

84696663R00092